TYPEN

GOOD, BAD AND UGLY HOUSES

Oda Pälmke
mit/with Rabea Köster

jovis

Autorin/Author: Oda Pälmke
Mitarbeit/In collaboration with: Rabea Köster

Umschlag und Satz/Cover and setting: Stephan Müller, Berlin
Druck und Bindung/Printing and binding: Pinguin Druck, Berlin

Bibliografische Information der Deutschen Bibliothek
Die Deutsche Bibliothek verzeichnet diese Publikation in der Deutschen Nationalbibliografie; detaillierte bibliografische Daten sind im Internet über http://dnb.ddb.de abrufbar./ Bibliographic information published by Die Deutsche Bibliothek; Die Deutsche Bibliothek lists this publication in the Deutsche National-bibliografie; detailed bibliographic data are available on the Internet at http://dnb.ddb.de

jovis Verlag
Kurfürstenstraße 15/16
DE-10785 Berlin
www.jovis.de

ISBN 978-3-86859-000-5

Die abgebildeten Modelle entstanden 2006-2008 als Ergebnisse zu dem Aufgabenzyklus: „Entwerfe das Haus!" im Rahmen der Vorlesungsreihe: „Idee Idee Idee!" am Lehrstuhl Grundlagen der Architektur, TU Dortmund.

Vertretende Lehrstuhlleitung Dipl. Ing. Oda Pälmke
Wissenschaftliche Mitarbeit Dipl. Ing. Rabea Köster

Dieses Buch wurde ermöglicht durch die Fakultät Architektur, Städtebau und Bauingenieurswesen Technische Universität Dortmund

The models presented were made from 2006-2008 as the results of the assignment cycle titled, "Design the house!" in the context of the lecture series, "Idee Idee Idee!" at the Fundamentals of Architecture chair of the TU Dortmund.

Acting head of chair: Dipl. Ing. Oda Pälmke
Academic collaboration: Dipl. Ing. Rabea Köster

This book was enabled by the Faculty of Architecture, Urban Planning and Engineering at the Technical University Dortmund

Oda Pälmke

TYPEN

GOOD, BAD AND UGLY HOUSES

jovis

GOOD, BAD AND UGLY HOUSES

Oda Pälmke

Models of houses, which are presented as types in the various senses of the word, can be considered here in typological-morphological series; archetypes and very special types as well as curious figures or "odd ducks". As test pieces of prospective architects, they represent altercations with multi-faceted spatial-functional issues concerning the "house".

The basic task of architecture, the "normal house", has been tested and put into practice in model experiments. Each of the houses shown represents an attempt to bring ideal and reality into unison. The diversity of design solutions develops through an interplay of intuitive and rational decisions. It is remarkable that the regional-cultural backgrounds of the young designers as well as their personal experience often remained at the forefront of their attempts to shape this archetype and to iconographically extend it. The search for a valid form moved between a likeness of the familiar (reality) and an idea of the novel (ideal) – an extremely subjectively-motivated balancing act through which architectural quality can be discovered or invented, sometimes unintentionally.

In the series presented here, the absolutely solid house is to be understood as a sculpture; it has been taken out of its design context and is presented as a type, isolated and without reference to place. It can be traced back only to itself and objectified; it demonstrates a more or less typical or specific solution without compre-

GOOD, BAD AND UGLY HOUSES

Oda Pälmke

In typologisch-morphologischer Reihe können hier Modelle von Häusern betrachtet werden, die sich als Typen in den verschiedenen Bedeutungen des Wortes vorstellen: Sowohl Archetypen als auch ganz spezielle Typen, merkwürdige Gestalten oder auch „komische Vögel". Als Probestücke angehender Architekten sind sie Auseinandersetzungen mit den vielfältigen räumlich-funktionalen Fragestellungen zum Thema „Haus".
Im Modellversuch wird die grundlegende Aufgabe der Architektur geprobt und realisiert: das „normale Haus". Jedes der gezeigten Häuser steht für den Versuch, Ideal und Wirklichkeit in Einklang zu bringen. Die Vielfalt der entwurflichen Problemlösungen entwickelt sich im Wechselspiel von intuitiven und rationalen Entscheidungen. Hier ist bemerkenswert, dass der regional-kulturelle Hintergrund und die persönliche Erfahrung der jungen Verfasser bei dem Versuch, den Archetyp zu formen und ikonografisch zu erweitern, vielfach im Vordergrund stehen. Die Suche nach einer gültigen Form bewegt sich zwischen dem Abbild des Gekannten (Wirklichkeit) und der Idee des Neuen (Ideal) – ein äußerst subjektiv motivierter Balanceakt, über den manchmal auch unbeabsichtigt eine architektonische Qualität erfunden oder herausgefunden wird.
In der hier präsentierten Reihe ist das als Skulptur verstandene, absolut gesetzte Haus aus seiner entwurflichen Fragestellung herausgenommen und wird als Typ, isoliert und ohne Ortsbezug, dargestellt. Es wird auf sich

hensive explanations of the demands that it is based upon. A group of characteristics or an essential feature is expressed in this reduced depiction of what characterises a house and of what accords its morphological quality. However, the pure form is positioned at the beginning of the design process instead of at the end, as would be normal. It gives expression to the originality and also to the essence of the design, without it necessarily being complete.

The observer is given the opportunity and also the imperative to think the house to the end in correspondence to its design logic and sketched semiotic character. This futherthinking of the form also implies involvement with the perceivable more or less complex structures of the rooms or space inside the house.

The models are not sorted according to space, time, scale or function but rather, without judgement, according to their essential characteristics and features. In the typological-morphological series presented, they simulate a neighbourhood in which the extreme is located beside the balanced and is able to exist there - and naturally vice-versa. This sorting preserves interest in the insufficiencies, the right wrong answers, snapshots in a search for the ideal.

Special types, complete with their deformations and irregularities, have been incorporated into the series of archetypes striving towards perfection. Odd characters are just as much to be found as are harmonious beauties; a portrait gallery that would not be complete without its striking features in which the representative and the random, the ugly and the beautiful, the boastful and

selbst zurückgeführt, objektiviert, und demonstriert eine mehr oder weniger typische oder spezifische Lösung ohne umfassende Erläuterung der zugrunde liegenden Anforderungen. In der reduzierten Darstellung ist entweder eine Gruppe von Eigenschaften oder auch nur ein wesentliches Merkmal zum Ausdruck gebracht, welches das Haus charakterisiert und ihm morphologische Qualität verleiht. Die einfache Form steht hier allerdings nicht, wie sonst üblich, am Ende des Entwurfsprozesses, sondern am Anfang. In ihr ist die Ursprünglichkeit, aber auch die Essenz des Entwurfes zur Aussage gebracht, ohne dass dieser dazu notwendigerweise vollendet ist. Dem Betrachter bleibt somit die Möglichkeit, aber auch die Notwendigkeit, das Haus entsprechend seiner entwurflichen Logik und skizzierten Zeichenhaftigkeit „zu Ende zu denken". Dieses Weiterdenken der Form bedeutet die gleichzeitige Auseinandersetzung mit der zu erahnenden, mehr oder weniger komplexen Struktur der Räume oder des Raumes im Inneren des Hauses.
Die Modelle sind nicht räumlich, zeitlich, maßstäblich oder funktional, sondern lediglich anhand ihrer wesentlichen Eigenschaften und Merkmale und ohne Wertung sortiert. In der dargebotenen typologisch-morphologischen Reihe simulieren sie eine Nachbarschaft, in der das Extreme neben dem Ausgeglichenen steht und auch bestehen kann – und natürlich auch umgekehrt. Diese Sortierung bewahrt sich das Interesse an den Unzulänglichkeiten, den richtigen falschen Antworten, den Momentaufnahmen auf der Suche nach dem Ideal. So sind die speziellen Typen mit ihren Deformationen und Abweichungen eingegliedert in die Reihe der nach

the modest, the loud and the quiet are made available to the interested observer for comparative examination. All of them are positively motivated results in search of happiness; judgement of the individual is left to the observer. Recognition of things already known or experienced does not remain absent, enriching the interpretation of the presented types.

A choreography of fine displacements and deviations emerges from the groupings; apart from a few exceptions the buildings do not make any great gestures. Narrative association connects the houses into pairs, groups and figures standing in relation to each other as a result of the distance between them, whose characteristics and building parts make reference to each other with no necessary formal concord. This narrative neighbourhood line enriches and defines the reading matter and perhaps the way in which each individual house is read, opening the further possibility to discover the remarkable in the manifold curiosities of life. Perception is thus sensitised in an undogmatic manner, the view of reality is sharpened and ultimately the imagination of the observer is broadened.

Vollkommenheit strebenden Archetypen. Merkwürdige Charaktere finden sich ebenso wie harmonische Schönheiten: Eine Porträtgalerie, die ohne Charakterköpfe nicht vollständig wäre, in der das Repräsentative ebenso wie das Beiläufige, das Hässliche wie das Schöne, das Prahlerische wie das Bescheidene, das Laute wie das Leise dem interessierten Betrachter zur vergleichenden Untersuchung zur Verfügung gestellt werden. Allesamt sind sie positiv motivierte Ergebnisse auf der Suche nach dem Glück, die Bewertung des Einzelnen bleibt dem Betrachter überlassen. Ein Wiedererkennen von bereits Gesehenem und Erlebtem bleibt natürlich nicht aus und bereichert die Interpretation der vorgestellten Typen.
In der Gruppierung ergibt sich eine Choreografie feiner Verschiebungen und Abweichungen, bis auf wenige Ausnahmen zeigen die Gebäude keine großen Gesten. Über narrative Assoziation verbinden sich die Häuser zu Hauspaaren, Gruppen und aus der Distanz zueinander in Beziehung stehenden Figuren, deren Eigenschaften und Bauteile ohne notwendige formale Übereinstimmung aufeinander verweisen. Diese erzählerische Linie der Nachbarschaft bereichert und bestimmt die Lektüre, vielleicht sogar die Lesart jedes einzelnen Hauses und eröffnet die weitergehende Möglichkeit, in den mannigfaltigen Merkwürdigkeiten von Realität das Bemerkenswerte zu entdecken. Auf undogmatische Weise mag so die Wahrnehmung sensibilisiert, der Blick auf die Realität geschärft und letztendlich die Phantasie des Betrachters erweitert werden.

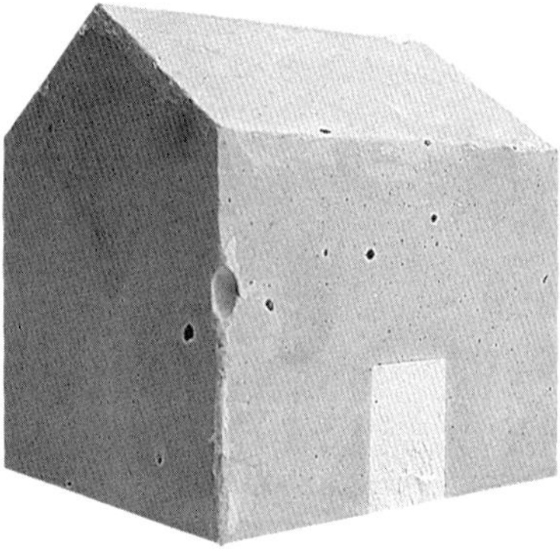

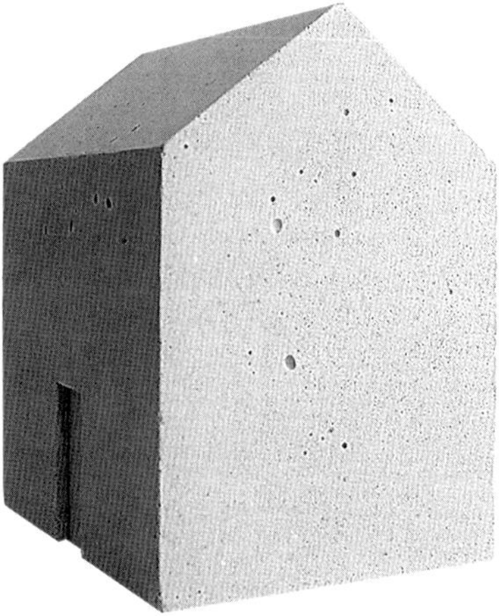

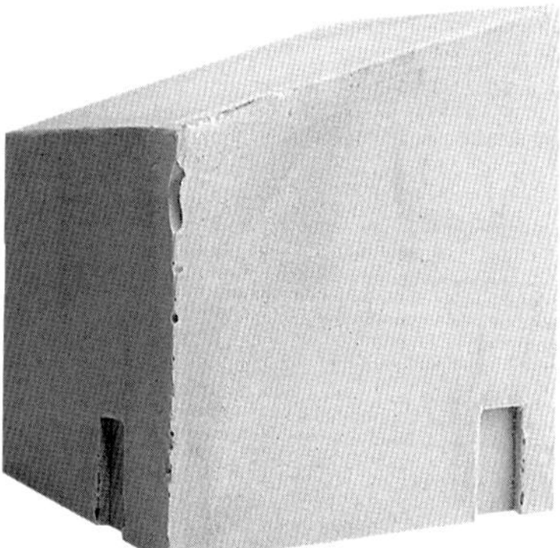

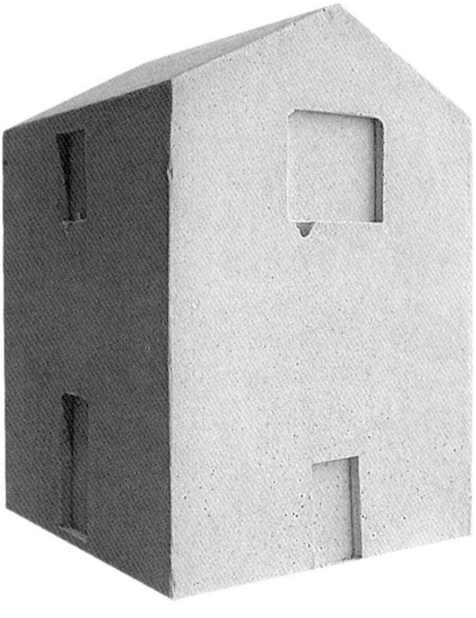

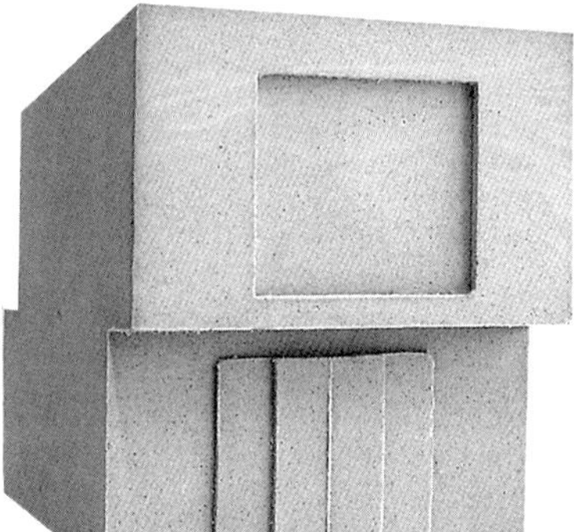

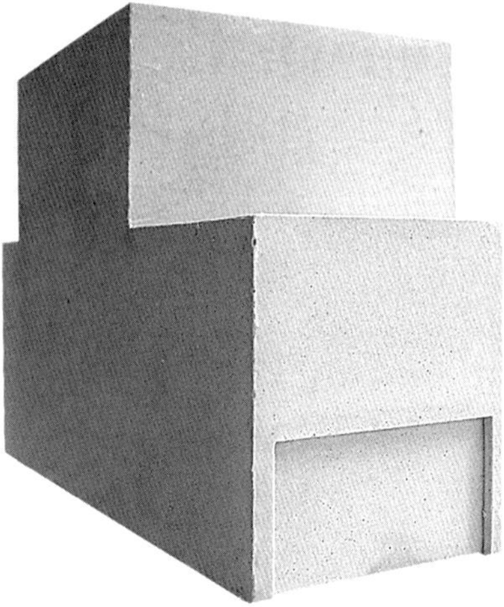

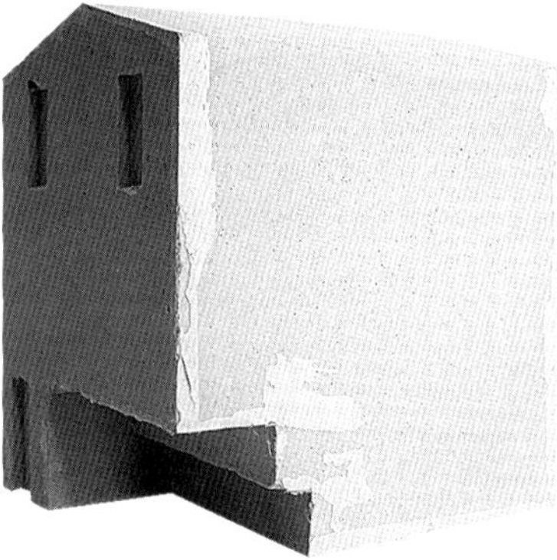

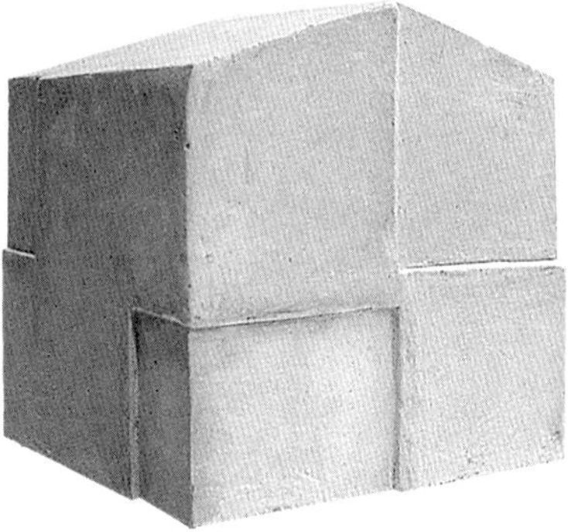

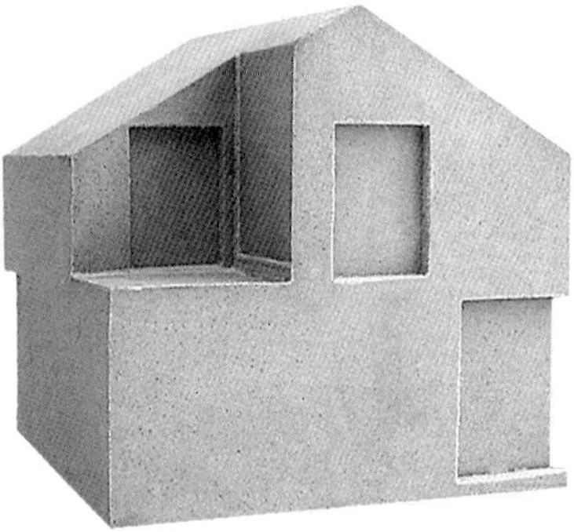

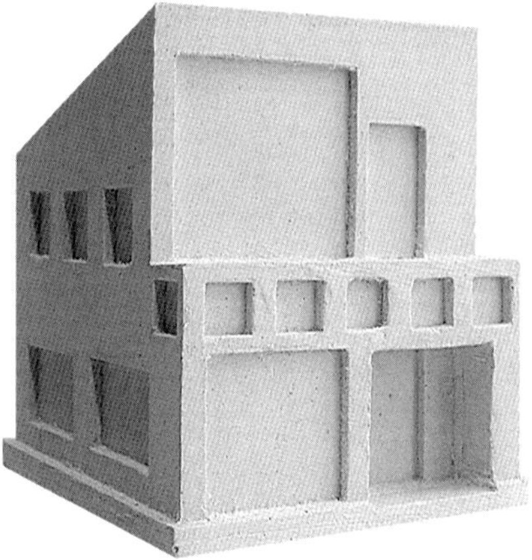

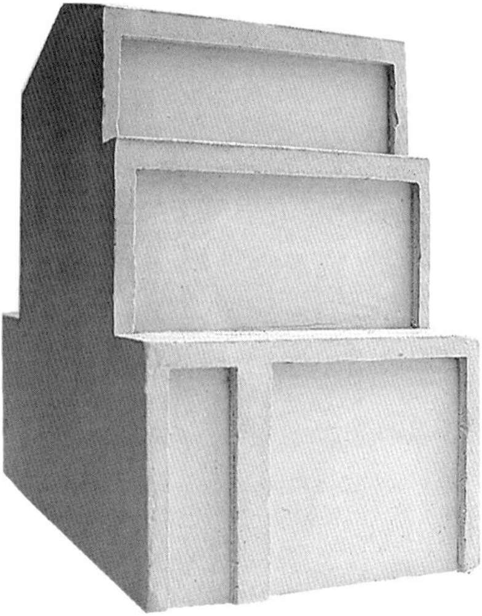

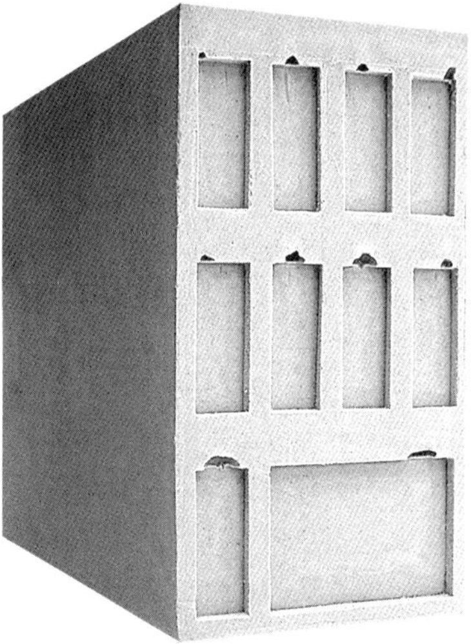

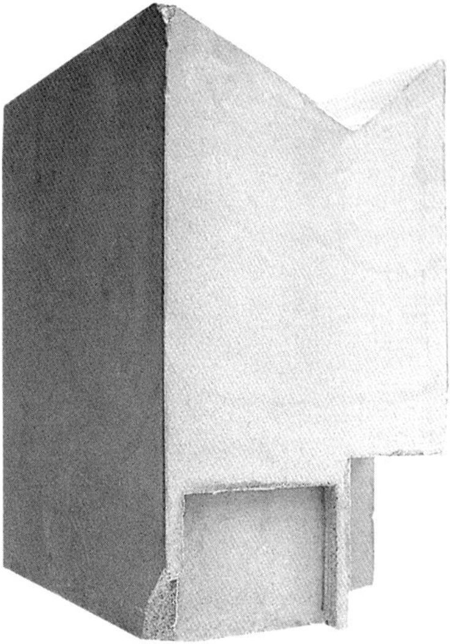

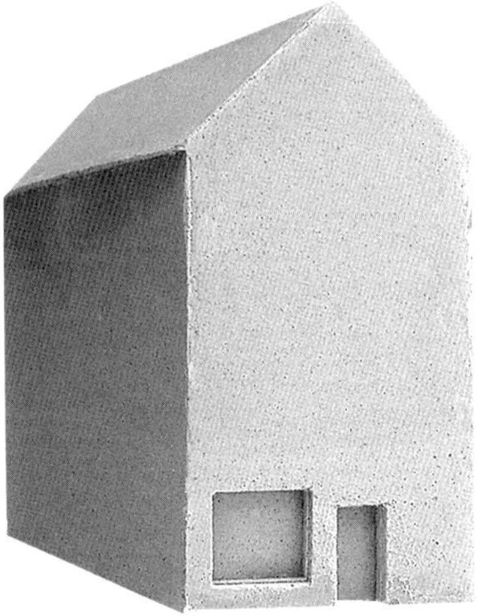

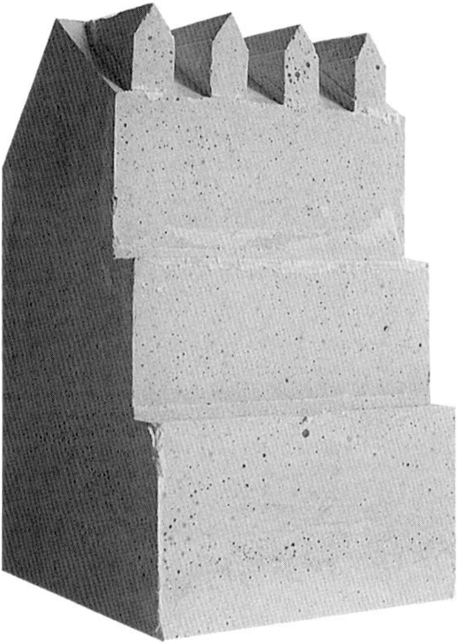

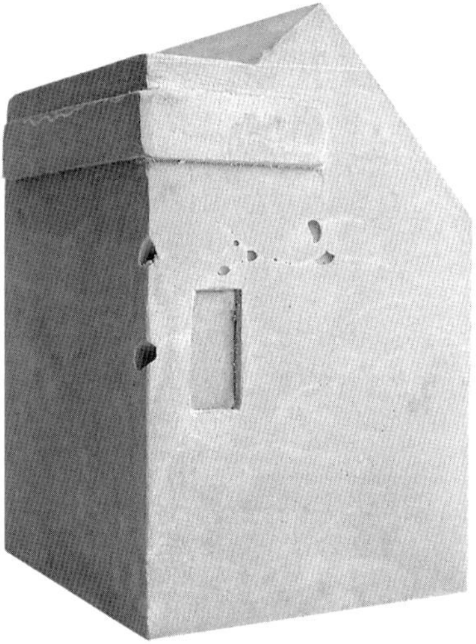

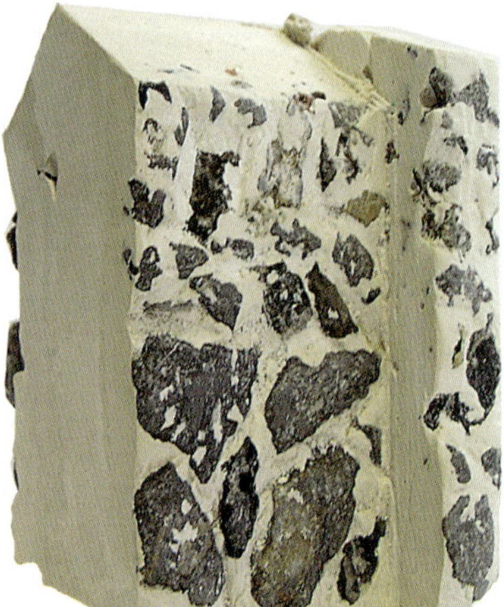

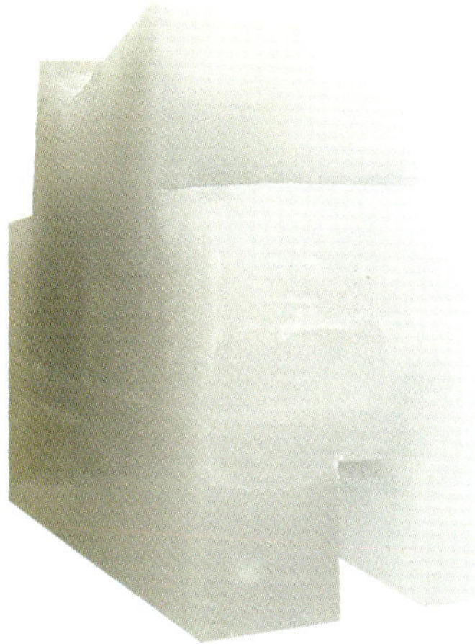

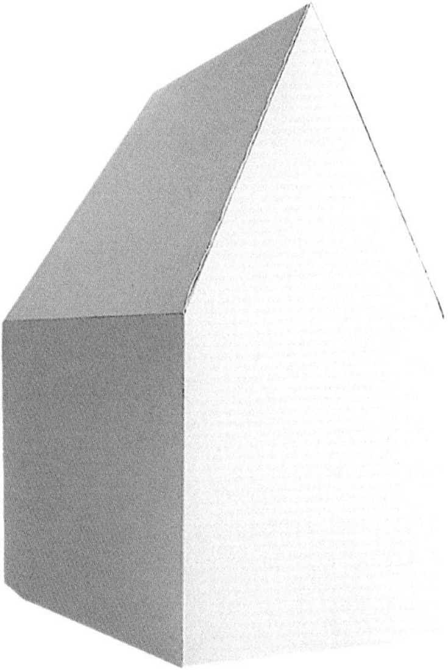

Vielen Dank

Faten Abdeli, Dunja Abood, Nedzada Ahmetspahic, Marzena Ambroziak, Al Khalaf Ammar, Nikola Atanasov, Isabel Baasner, Natalie Baron, Joscha Bell, Henning Bergmann, Sarah Bester, Katharina Bienia, Achim Bock, Matthias Bockstruck, Ramona Böhlke, Nils Bollmann, Michael Bouecke, Souad Boujloud, Eva Brockhoff, Selma Brulic, Anais Buß, Fulya Cakir, Ali Chaer, Elyes Chaouch, Damla Cicek, Sina Czempik, Yesim Dalmaz, Xinyu Deng, Gülten Denir, Jan Dienstknecht, Noel Dirani, Fabian Dirkes, Sven Dürre, Jana Eggenstein, Matthias Eicher, Sarah Engelhardt, Paola Esser, Elisa Feistel, Yvonne Fiestelmann, Simona Filcheva, Claudia Focking, Niclas Foth, Alexandra Förster, Sabrina Fried, Andrea Friehs, Madita Fritsch, Peter Frohn, Tanja Füllbier, Thomas Furtak, Kerstin Gabrisch, Chimene Gaspar, Maria Gazani, Eugenia Glaschockowa, Magdalena A. Gnojczak, Stephanie Göb, Ann-Kathrin Goerke, Abdulkadir Gökcen, Jeremia Gonzales Martinez, Inna Gorval, Sarah Go-un Balke, Martin Grasse, Tatjana Gretschannikow, Tobias Greuel, Judith Grobusch, Katarzyna Grocholski, Mandy Hahn, Tim Hanke, Christina Hassa, Trine Hausmann, Julie Henkel, Katharina Hentschel, Alexander Herlich, Natalie Hoffmann, Max Hofmann, Jana Hohmann, Miriam Honnacker, Christian Honstein, Damian Hoy, Emilie Janik, Annika Jobs, Anna Katharina Jost, Thorsten Alexander Kaja, Katrin Kalnik, Ali-Can Karasu, Valentina Karsten, Slawomir Kazmierski, Maryam Kefayati, Sascha Kerkhoff, Julia Kettschau, Ibrahim Kilic, Marcel Klegin, Manuela Kletzel, Tobias Knorn, Ben Koch, Marie-Therese

Kocken, Jens Kothe, Chris Korpilla, Tim Kramer, Monika Krawczyk, Johannes Kriegisch, Marian Krüger, Tessa Kücke, Philipp Kühnapfel, Tim Kujat, Mareike Kuhn, Marius Kunz, Jessica Kurreck, Katharina Kuzmann, Theresa Lang, Larissa Lange, Henrike Langer, Marie-Fleur Langhans, Joscha Lenz, Shuo Li, Dorothea Lipinski, Kristina Lorrek, Linda Luhmann, Milena Macha, Heela Mangal, Adam Materla, Roland Meinzer, Matthias Mertens, Ermina Mesanaic, Friederike Michels, Sylvia Miklosovic, Jasmin Milosevic, Sarah Moell, Nils Moldenhauer, Baland Mohammad, Zoran Mrsic, Manuel Mueller, Sonja Niggemeier, Marina Nikolova, Maren Oberholz, Tim Osthoff, Beata Pacer, Karen Panek, Sarah Perlitz, Christopher Peters, Maximilian Pflichtenhöfer, Dima Popova, Viola Potberg, Sarah Rahim, Christoph Reichel, Martin Rohrbach, Raphael Roth, Matthias Rügge, Johann Rump, Sina Scheele, Edda Scheffler, Anja Schiller, Alexander Schirjajew, Kerstin Iris Schneider, Patrick Schreiber, Jannic Schubert, Dominik Schürmann, Aydin Sener, Stefan Setzer, Karsten Siebel, Adrian Simut, Sebastian Spengler, Annalena Spinks, Sina Sternberg, Emil Tanev, Resul Tekinbas, Roman Tesch, Sabrina Tschuden, Katharina Tschursin, Frank Tuchtenhagen, Sebastian Viehoff, Dimitrij Vinogradskij, Stefan Vlahov, Jan Vogels, Simone Wagner, Malte Wagner, Yi Ting Wang, Lisa Wawrzyniak, Alexander Weber, Melanie Wehner, Kevin Weidemann, Nadine Weigl, Matthias Welp, Monique Westrich, Anastasia Wittich, Karen Wolf, Carola Wolters, Judith Wotzka, Chen Yining, Roja Zaitoonie, Martin Ziegenhagen